build your
CONFIDENCE

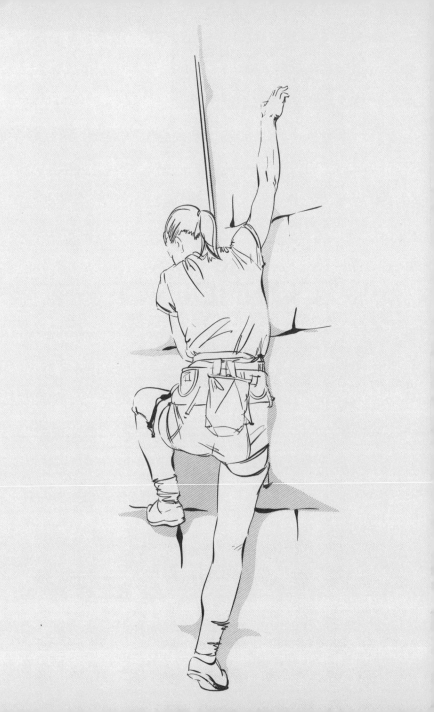

build your
CONFIDENCE

Use mindfulness and meditation
to boost self-esteem

Includes
audio
meditation

TARA WARD

ARCTURUS

ARCTURUS

This edition published in 2020 by Arcturus Publishing Limited
26/27 Bickels Yard, 151–153 Bermondsey Street,
London SE1 3HA

ISBN: 978-1-83857-759-9
AD007962UK

Printed in China

CONTENTS

INTRODUCTION

Welcome! Increasing your confidence is a great goal to have, because it will help you to enjoy every aspect of life more fully. And because people seem to learn best when they are having a good time, you are going to 'play' as you go through each step, using fun and insightful exercises.

Of course, confidence means different things to different people, so this book is going to be a personal journey to help you determine what it looks and feels like for you. The experiences you have as you discover a new-found confidence will be unique to you.

I'm going to encourage you to delve inside yourself to understand where your lack of confidence began, so we can work from the beginning and 'build you up', so to speak. This will ensure that the confidence you feel is genuine, not a superficial top layer with uncertainties still bubbling away underneath.

You may find some steps more helpful than others, but I suggest that you go through each stage to make sure you are creating a holistic experience of confidence that makes you feel good physically, emotionally, mentally and spiritually.

Also, at the end of each step you'll find an account of my own experience of creating more confidence in my life. It's an up-and-down journey and I hope my honesty will help you in your own growth.

Before you start reading the first step, please take a look at the Confidence Plan which starts on page 118. Filling this in as you go through the steps will help to keep you motivated and make sure you stay on track.

Right, let's get started!

HELPFUL HINTS

I've sprinkled hints throughout the steps. Some are light-hearted, others deeper. Have a play with them and see if they help you.

Step 1

. . . .

Contemplating
Confidence

I promised you fun during this journey into confidence, so we are going to start straight away by playing a mind-freeing 'game'.

Take a large sheet of paper and in the middle write the word 'confidence'. Now, without stopping to think too deeply, start drawing arrows out of the word and at the end of each arrow, write down what confidence means to you.

There is no right or wrong answer – just let your mind run free without censoring it. See it as a fun game where you can do whatever you want; write as many words as you want, and nothing is good or bad. Take your time.

No one is going to judge you and no one has to see this piece of paper but you. Scribble away for as long as you like. You might find yourself writing some things you weren't expecting; that is fine. When you have run out of steam, stop and review what you have written. You might want to circle certain things that really resonate with you. Admire your artwork.

HELPFUL HINT

Why not use coloured pens or pencils with this?
Choose a bright sheet of paper.
Make it look good.

Put the paper away for a little while and then return to it. Consider it more closely. This reflects how you feel about confidence right now in your life. Notice how many things you have written that you find encouraging and helpful.

Look at the way you have written the word 'confidence' itself. Is it in large or small letters? How much of the paper does it cover? How firm was your pressure as you wrote? As you study your sheet, decide what it says about your attitude to confidence. Then note down your findings under Step 1 in your Confidence Plan. It doesn't matter whether you find your thoughts positive or negative; write them all down.

Now let's consider what others have decided the word 'confidence' means. Look it up in different dictionaries; what do you find? Which definition do you like the best, and why? 'Confidence' can mean several things, ranging from believing in someone or something to telling someone a private matter. Both of these definitions are going to be useful for us during this journey – you will see why in Step 3. Experiencing confidence is much more than telling yourself you are confident, or having others think you are confident, despite you feeling unsure inside. The true state of confidence is feeling comfortable no matter what is happening to you in life.

There are times when it is easier for us to feel a degree of confidence. For instance, having a rewarding job, enjoying healthy relationships with family and friends and feeling useful to others can all engender a feeling of self-worth that makes us feel good.

But having self-worth and feeling useful or powerful are not necessarily going to give you great confidence. After all, there are plenty of famous performers, rich, successful and adored by many, who are still unconfident.

So I want to help you take this 'confidence' experience to a much deeper level, where your bubble of feeling good isn't burst by outside influences, but is a deep core within you that cannot be shaken.

There is considerable debate over whether confidence is a result of nature or nurture: are our genes responsible or is our upbringing more influential? The general

consensus seems to be that we are affected by both, but the percentages vary a great deal. However, irrespective of the nature/nurture ratio, we are going to examine how to increase your confidence levels based on how you feel right now.

So once you have 'played' with the word 'confidence' on paper, let's take it deeper with a mini-meditation. You have the choice of reading through this meditation and then trying it, or you may wish to listen to my voice talking you through the process. The link to download the latter is here (http://delivr.com/2cqjn).

HELPFUL HINT

You don't need to try too hard in this exercise. The more relaxed and comfortable you are, the easier it is to do, so spend a little time unwinding first.

STEP 1:
THE 'CONFIDENCE' MEDITATION

Please make sure you have at least ten minutes to do this, where you can be alone and won't be disturbed. You want to be relaxed before you start this confidence meditation, so why not do this in a fun way? Put on a favourite piece of music and have a little dance or sing along. Enjoy a relaxing scent: lavender or geranium are wonderful soothers. Or simply take time to lie down, close your eyes, breathe deeply and feel your body relax and your mind stop whirling. Focus on different parts of your body and feel them become heavy: legs, arms, torso, neck and head. To quieten your mind, try slowly counting up to ten.

When you feel pleasantly relaxed and are lying in a comfortable position, with your eyes closed, you are ready to focus on something specific.

Write the word 'confidence' in large letters in front of you, in your mind's eye. Make it very clear. Look at the word and then absorb it into you. Imagine swallowing the word, or picture it entering into your body.

How does that make you feel? How does it differ from what you wrote on your paper? Let yourself 'digest' the experience. Play with the feeling of it being inside you: let the word expand and contract. Have it become bright and pulsing, then let it diminish. See it as different colours.

How do they make you feel? Imagine the word as very glittery; see it sparkling. Take your time. Notice how you feel. Let the word fade, become smaller and smaller, and finally see it disappear into nothingness.

Now you are going to do something different. Take your mind to a time in your life when you felt supremely confident. It might be when you were praised for something, or when you accomplished a difficult task, or when you won a prize. Take a moment to choose your experience. Make sure it is one where you felt really confident.

Now allow yourself to remember it fully; totally embrace the sensation and feel yourself entering into it all, as if it were happening all over again right now. How is your body feeling? Find the right adjectives to describe it. What emotions are you feeling right now? What sound personifies this moment? What smell or taste goes with it? What do you see in your mind's eye? Wallow in how good it feels. You may find yourself smiling or laughing or wanting to say something. Indulge yourself. Kick your heels or punch the air; do whatever feels good from your relaxed position.

Let your eyes remain closed to keep the sensations intense.

When you feel you have truly immersed yourself in this experience, slowly bring your attention back to your physical body and realize that it feels heavy and relaxed. Give a gentle stretch. Yawn if you wish. Slowly open your eyes and focus on an object in the room before you get up.

Then fill in your experience of this meditation in your Confidence Plan while it is still fresh in your mind. Pay particular attention to the adjectives you want to use and the images/sounds/smells/tastes/sensations which came to mind.

So how did you find this first mini-meditation? Hopefully, you are still experiencing the feeling of confidence, although this sensation will be different for everyone because people respond in individual ways. You might feel quite 'buzzy' now or wonderfully calm and serene; perhaps you just feel very peaceful. Whatever you feel is personal and right for you.

PERSONAL EXAMPLE

After writing this section, I decided to redraw my Confidence Sheet. I love colours, so I used plenty of them! I have worked on my own level of confidence for a long time now and I was interested to see that I still had some critical words within my drawing, indicating that I felt there was more improvement possible. I think it shows that, however much we work on ourselves, there is always more we can do.

Step 2

. . . .

Fearing Confidence

This may sound strange, but there are reasons why you might fear feeling confident. Living in a state of confidence inevitably means we begin to see ourselves and others in a different light. That can be unsettling.

Sometimes we hide behind an 'Oh, that isn't possible' attitude, because while we are clinging to that, we don't need to change. It can be easier to complain than to do something about our situation. We may not always like what we are experiencing, but it is familiar and we learn to become comfortable within that sphere. Breaking out can feel scary. In other words, what might you have to give up in order to accept confidence?

You're going to go a bit deeper with this next meditation but, as always, you will find the opportunity to play within it, so you can enjoy yourself too.

HELPFUL HINT

Enter into the spirit of this meditation by remembering what you loved to play when you were a child. Can you remember the feeling of fun and excitement as you started a favourite game? Carry that energy with you now.

STEP 2:
THE 'HOW NOT TO FEAR CONFIDENCE' MEDITATION

Close your eyes and take a few deep, comfortable breaths. Make sure you are sitting or lying in a relaxing position.

Now allow yourself to concentrate on an area of your life in which you do NOT feel confident. Avoid choosing a major issue for your first time; instead select something small but one that is relevant for you.

Don't spend time delving into the emotion of this issue but do ask yourself, 'What do I gain from feeling unconfident about this?' Notice it is not about trying to find reasons for your lack of confidence so that you can justify it. This is about you accepting there are reasons why you CHOOSE to feel as you do. What is the benefit of having your attitude to this issue? Be honest with yourself. There is always a benefit.

For example: you might feel unconfident if asked to speak in front of a large group of people. By refraining from doing this, you never have to

worry about finding your own 'voice' or expressing who you are; you avoid potential rejection or criticism. Do you see how this works?

Question yourself quite thoroughly over how you benefit from your lack of confidence in your chosen area. Spend time looking at all the possibilities as they may not be obvious. As you do so, start to imagine yourself in a cage, shut off from all these potential experiences, because of your perceived lack of confidence. As you consider every conceivable 'benefit' from staying unsure of yourself, see the 'benefits' piling up around your cage.

Now a strange thing will begin to happen. As more 'benefits' heap up around you, you will start to feel frustrated. It is a small feeling inside that slowly begins to grow. You are in a cage that you have decided to build for yourself. You are now heaping up obstacles around you that mean you are even more trapped. It isn't what you want. You begin to feel that the situation is ridiculous.

What are you doing in this cage? Perhaps you thought you would feel comfortable and safe in here but instead you are beginning to feel hemmed in and dissatisfied. You want out.

Now notice your body shape is changing. Your human shape is becoming an animal. Watch as you find yourself morphing into the energy of a large, strong creature. Are you a lion? An elephant? A rhinoceros? Let yourself become this animal and, as you do so, effortlessly pull apart the bars of the cage and step out. Look at all the obstacles around you and realize you don't want or need any of them. Crush them underfoot, until they become nothing but dust.

When you have finished, you will shake your head in wonderment at not doing this sooner; now you are ready to discover your next cage and obstacles and to destroy them too.

But instead of doing this, begin to disconnect from your animal. Slowly bring your focus back into your human body; acknowledge your very human shape. Notice it feels heavy and solid. Wait a few minutes before opening your eyes and then focus on a solid object in the room.

Sit up slowly, and remember to fill in Step 2 of your Confidence Plan before you get up.

How has this meditation left you feeling? You might be surprised, realizing that some of your behaviour has been a means of escaping a challenge in life. Perhaps there are several challenges. Of course those challenges are also opportunities that you are denying yourself. How do you react to that? How did it make you feel as you pulverized those excuses?

Reflect also on how it felt to be that strong, powerful animal. What creature did you become? Why? What does it mean to you?

You can return to this meditation whenever you wish, to look at other areas in which you feel unconfident. You might find you are different animals for different situations. Notice how your resolve grows stronger with each meditation and how good it feels to be that animal.

PERSONAL EXAMPLE

When I was younger, I didn't believe in this step. My whole attitude was one of, 'I will say I am strong and confident and that will make me so.' It took me many, many years to realize that what I was saying and what I was feeling inside were two totally different things. I was building up a brittle shell of supposed confidence, while inside I still felt vulnerable and inadequate, even though I didn't want to admit it.

Step 3

. . . .

Invoking Your Confidence

Here is a little secret for you. In fact, it's a BIG secret and one that we are going to spend this step discussing. Deep inside, in our inner core (or in our soul, if you prefer that terminology) we are confident already. Being confident isn't something we have to learn, it is something we have to rediscover. In other words, we need to invoke it. I've alluded to this already, but now we are ready to look at this fact in more detail.

Remember that in Step 1, I said that definitions of confidence in dictionaries include believing in someone or something as well as telling someone something private. I believe this is actually the same thing.

We can believe in ourselves and have confidence, and to do that we have to keep reminding a secret part inside us that we are confident. The way to do this is to access that true state of confidence within us and to become good friends with it.

It's important to understand that confidence isn't about receiving approbation from others, or from situations, in order to make us feel good. You can be the richest, most powerful person in the world, but that doesn't mean you are truly confident. It just means others may be fooled into thinking you are.

Residing in the real state of confidence means that, whatever happens to you, whatever life throws at you, you know you can handle it. In fact, you won't even question it. This is the massive benefit waiting for you. Some people only learn how to embrace this truth when they are faced with terrible difficulties and slowly, painfully, they learn the hard way what confidence really is. We are going to make your journey much easier and more pleasant!

So how can you experience and get to know this inner core of confidence?

It might help to have a visual image. Think of a stone inside a piece of fruit. The stone itself is the core, the essence, and around it grows the edible outer fruit that may be hard or soft, sweet or bitter. While the outer part can be treated in any way – sliced, squashed, eaten or destroyed – the hard inner seed remains and is not easy to destroy. Consider your confidence as that seed inside you. Outer parts of you may have all sorts of experiences, both nice and not so nice, but only they can be manipulated. Your inner, confident core remains strong and unmoveable.

Have that concept in mind as you try the next meditation.

HELPFUL HINT

This meditation can go to a deep level but remember that you choose how far you want to go. As long as you are enjoying the experience, keep going. If you feel uncomfortable, pull back. You are in charge.

STEP 3:
THE 'INVOKING YOUR CORE OF CONFIDENCE' MEDITATION

You need to be alone and undisturbed, so find the right time for this meditation. I prefer to sit up; you might decide to lie down. Close your eyes and allow yourself to relax for a while. Breathe deeply. Imagine your lungs are way down at the base of your spine and breathe into that area of your body. Feel each breath lengthen and deepen. Notice how good it feels.

When you are comfortable, contemplate the image of a seed in a piece of fruit. Do you like that as an image for your inner core of confidence? If you don't, choose something that feels right for you. It might be a ball of colour, a smooth stone or a symbol. Take your time. Whisper the word 'core of confidence' or even 'my confidence' as you explore your options. When you find the right image, you will know. You will connect with it and feel a sense of strength simply from 'seeing' it. Now become more familiar with your chosen image or symbol. What size is it? What colour and shape?

What material? Does it have a sound, smell, taste or feeling associated with it? Take your time. How do you feel as you strengthen your connection with your image?

Once you feel you know your image/symbol really well and are comfortable with it, imagine it going into your body and see where it would like to be. It can move around, as you will discover later, but there will always be a natural abode, a location where it will reside most of the time.

This can be anywhere in your body and there is no right or wrong place. Everyone has to find their own personal location. You may find your image sliding around your body as it finds the place. This is a very pleasant experience; enjoy it.

When its natural home is found, you will feel it. It might manifest as a 'click' or a slight jolt. You may feel a profound sense of peace or contentment. You might want to pat the area of your body in which it has chosen to reside and notice how good it feels.

Now you want to take your attention away from your inner core of confidence and focus again on the material world around you. Become aware that your body feels heavy and relaxed. Wiggle your fingers and toes. Slowly open your eyes and survey what is around you. Choose an object upon which to focus and reorient yourself.

Once you are grounded again, sit up slowly and then make a note of what you experienced on Step 3 of your Confidence Plan.

Discovering this inner core of confidence is a profound experience and can be life-changing. Often we can be fooled into thinking that if only certain things would happen to us, we would become confident. Learning that we control that feeling ourselves is a big breakthrough. Take time to digest this step and what it means to you. Make sure you do this meditation a few times before you move on to Step 4.

PERSONAL EXAMPLE

I like to be in control – it's part of my nature – so before I started this meditation I decided I knew what my symbol of confidence would look like. It was going to be a small, smooth piece of green stone and it would reside somewhere around my navel area. I am not sure why I decided that was appropriate but for whatever reason, I had made up my mind. I spent some time relaxing and breathing deeply and then turned my focus towards a green stone. I was very surprised to see it flash before me and then, just as quickly, disappear into the ether.

I confess I felt a little peeved; I had been sure it was the best image for me. So then I had to let go of my irritation and allow myself to focus on whatever might be more appropriate. Nothing happened for a while and I began to feel impatient. Then a beautiful image slowly took shape in front of me. I knew immediately it was right. I found myself smiling and, as I did so, my connection with my image was cemented. We just 'clicked'.

Then again I tried to control the experience by placing it around my navel area. Once more I was thwarted, because it quickly bounced away and decided to place itself elsewhere. Resigned to letting it happen, I felt it settle into its new place and yet again I had that instant sensation of knowing it was right. This time I laughed out loud.

You see, although we sometimes try to convince ourselves we know what is best for us, we are at our most powerful when we let go and trust.

Conversely, I have had people say they have started this meditation, sure that nothing will happen, because they believe others may have this core of confidence, but that they are missing theirs. Just so you know, I've never come across anyone yet who hasn't found their own core.

Step 4

....

Dealing with Destructive Thoughts

You may have noticed by now that certain things are happening, or have happened, that have taken away some of your confidence. Sadly, many aspects of life can grind us down and make us feel less sure of ourselves. It won't necessarily stop happening, so we have to find a way to deal with it.

So let's acknowledge those demons right now; as we move forward, we want to have tools in place to handle those frustrating experiences. We're going to look at it in two ways: emotionally and physically. Let's look at the emotional aspect first.

STEP 4: THE 'DEALING WITH DESTRUCTIVE THOUGHTS' MEDITATION

Close your eyes and feel your body relaxing as you breathe deeply and easily. Do this for a few moments.

Now choose an example of where someone or something has made you lose confidence. Please choose a small issue for your first time; you can tackle larger problems later.

Focus on where this lack of confidence, or this destructive thought, is resting in your body. You may need a few minutes to work this out. Allow yourself to feel it. Accept that this feeling is real and genuine for you. You may find that it manifests itself physically and you can 'see' it or you may just sense it – that doesn't matter.

Now you want to shift your focus. Take your attention to where your symbol of confidence resides in you, as in your Step 3 meditation. Feel it glowing brightly within you. Allow yourself to connect with it and feel good. Next, take your symbol of confidence and shift it over to where

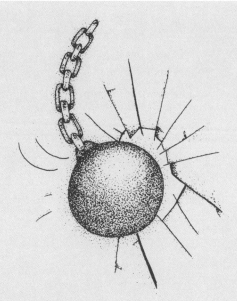

your unconfident emotion is residing at present. Yes, your symbol of confidence can travel to wherever you want it in your body! As you move it, notice something is happening. Your symbol of confidence is growing and as you place it over your unconfident feeling, the latter begins to diminish.

Remember that your confidence is a permanent part of you: it is your spirit and your soul. It cannot be destroyed. That feeling of not being confident, of being bruised or knocked emotionally, is just a destructive attitude you have held. It is an outer shell that can be removed whenever you are ready to let go. Are you ready now? Brush it away, break it up, feel it melt into nothingness — whatever image works for you.

The more you focus, the stronger your confidence becomes. If the destructive thoughts begin to creep back in, persevere. Don't let your brain take over and try to justify your feeling of inadequacy because there is no point. Simply keep focusing on your confidence, that true essence of you, because it will always 'win'. It is the natural part of you; all else is illusion.

This is worth saying: 'I am confident. All else is an illusion.' Notice how good it feels to say it. Repeat it. Mean it.

When you are ready, let your symbol of confidence slip back into the place in your body where it is at rest, and slowly bring your focus back into the world around you. Take a few minutes before you open your eyes and acknowledge where you are. Wait a few minutes before you get up and fill in Step 4 of your Confidence Plan.

So now you have a new way in which to access those destructive beliefs, to break them down and to rid yourself of them. Depending on the length of time you have had your negative emotions/experiences, you may need to return and to repeat your actions. It becomes easier each time you do it.

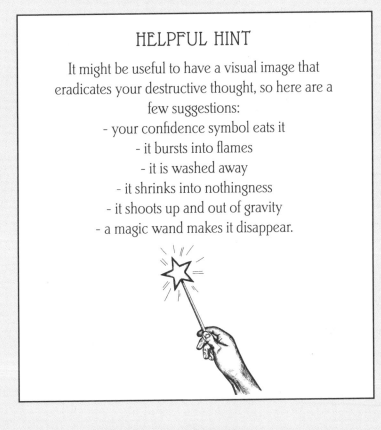

HELPFUL HINT

It might be useful to have a visual image that eradicates your destructive thought, so here are a few suggestions:
- your confidence symbol eats it
- it bursts into flames
- it is washed away
- it shrinks into nothingness
- it shoots up and out of gravity
- a magic wand makes it disappear.

Apart from looking at how we handle destructive thoughts using a mental tool, what we do physically with our body is an important factor too.

Our physical stance says a great deal about who we are. When you think of someone who appears unconfident, how do they stand or sit? Take a moment to jot down your thoughts. Conversely, when you see someone whom you would describe as supremely confident (but not arrogant), how would you describe them? Again, make notes of your thoughts.

When we feel unconfident, our shoulders tend to hunch forward and our head is lowered. Conversely, when we feel confident, our shoulders tend

to roll back in their sockets, our head is held up straight and our feet make equal contact with the ground.

To feel the difference for yourself, take a moment now to hunch over and lower your head. Let your body lean slightly to one side. How does it make you feel? Notice how squashed your lungs and ribcage are; it is impossible to breathe deeply in this position. How confident are you feeling?

Now lift your head, let your shoulders roll back in their sockets, plant both feet firmly on the floor and make sure your spine is upright and straight. How different do you feel now? How much easier is it to take a deep breath? Hold this position for a few more seconds.

Then let your body return to your natural physical shape. Where is your normal position in relation to a confident/unconfident pose? What does that say about you?

Many people hold themselves somewhere in between: neither comfortably upright nor hunched over. That is because most of us have a degree of confidence without going within to seek our truly natural state of confidence.

As you become more confident, as you become who you really are, notice how your body shape changes. It's a nice feeling. Practise holding yourself upright more often, even when you don't feel wonderful. That can help too.

Lastly, there are further physical things you can consider to help your confidence. They may be on a more superficial level, but they can still be useful. While I wouldn't suggest using only physical tools to help you become confident, a combination of mental and physical can work well.

Which colour, style and cut of clothes make you feel more confident? Which perfume and hairstyle? Does listening to a particular style of music or a certain singer make you feel confident? If certain people or symbols increase your confidence, can you find a way to have their energy around you, through images on your computer or phone or on the walls of your home?

When you feel you have explored enough of the options offered in this step, it's time to move on to Step 5.

PERSONAL EXAMPLE

I went through a difficult time with relationships in my late twenties. I came out of a long-term relationship and then within a few years found myself being rejected by a number of men, one after the other. It didn't make me feel great. Of course my confidence was eroded each time.

I knew I had to find a way forward and devised a few strategies. One that I found helpful (and still makes me smile today when I think of it) was to listen, and to sing along, to Gloria Gaynor's 'I Will Survive'. I had a fair amount of anger inside me about all those dismissals,

and when you belt out a song like that, it releases a heck of a lot of feeling. I highly recommend finding a song that works for you. Nowadays I tend to use my confidence symbol to go within and to tackle lack of confidence in that way. I also keep practising the 'standing up straight and feeling good about myself' physical stance. But I think that a combination of techniques, used for different situations at varying times in your life, is very useful.

Step 5

. . . .

Embracing
Confidence

So you have looked at what confidence means to you, imagined the joy of confidence, and learned how to banish destructive thoughts. Let's get on with truly embracing confidence now by putting together all the steps we have discussed so far. We'll kick off with a fun exercise. Please have a pen or pencil beside you when you start.

HELPFUL HINT

You might find some of these suggestions unusual. Allow yourself to 'play' in the safety of your own company and make sure you aren't going to be disturbed by anyone.

STEP 5:
THE 'EMBRACING CONFIDENCE' MINI-MEDITATION

Find a quiet, pleasant location in which to sit (not lie) comfortably. If you can find a decent-sized area for yourself, that will be ideal.

Start off by making sure you are sitting upright and ensure your spine is straight without feeling rigid. Have both feet planted firmly on the floor. Lift your head up, looking straight ahead of you. Roll your shoulders, then lift them up and let them fall.

Keeping your eyes open, focus on your symbol of confidence and where it resides inside you. Touch or pat it gently. Feel yourself smile. It's part of who you truly are. You don't need to have your eyes closed to concentrate on it.

Hum your confidence-inducing tune, if you wish; imagine the scent you like in your nostrils.

Now pick up your pen or pencil and place it lengthways in your mouth, holding it lightly between your teeth. Notice how it makes your lips curve upwards into a natural smile. It keeps you smiling.

Then get up and walk around the space you are in. Ensure your spine remains comfortably upright; keep your head up and your shoulders down. Periodically touch your body where your symbol of confidence resides and connect with it. Notice your feet feel solid and strong on the ground. You aren't trying to walk with confidence, you simply ARE confident.

Remove the pen or pencil from between your teeth and notice you want to continue smiling naturally.

Now stand still, remaining relaxed and upright. Begin to clap; clap into the air around you. Move slowly in a circle and clap all the air surrounding you. Realize as you do this that fragments of stale energy are being destroyed. You now feel cleaner and brighter and even more confident.

As you stand still again, realize there is a large animal by your side. It is one of your animals from Step 2. It makes you feel strong and secure. It is part of your own energy. Give it a pat if you wish. Notice you no longer need to become that animal because it is an outward symbol, a reminder, of what you already are.

When you are ready, return to your seat. Keeping your eyes open, reflect upon what you have just experienced. (You may find your animal follows and sits beside you. That is fine.)

When you are ready, make notes on your Confidence Plan about how you feel.

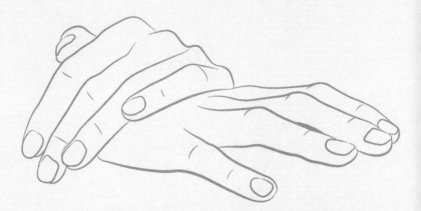

How confident did you feel after finishing this exercise? Confidence is a state of being, not doing, which is why this exercise is important. You don't need to tell yourself you are confident – you simply allow yourself to access that part of you that knows it already and to feel it as you go about your day.

You may not be familiar with the clapping technique, but it is very useful for releasing stuck energy around you. When we have moments of uncertainty and uncomfortableness, the energy from those emotions can stay in the ether around us and affect us, often on an unconscious level. Clapping it away literally clears the air, allowing our energy to flow more freely.

You may have found the pencil/pen between your teeth an interesting moment. It is something recommended by Dr Amy Cuddy in her wonderful TED talk, http://www.ted.com/talks/amy_cuddy_your_body_language_shapes_ who_you_are?language=en

Dr Cuddy talks about how physical poses affect your feeling of power. She claims that even if you don't feel powerful, standing in a powerful pose for just two minutes raises your testosterone levels and lowers those of your cortisol (dominance and stress hormones respectively). In other words, you can stand in a certain way, not even believing in the power of it, and your hormones will still respond – hence my advice that if you sit or stand with a straight spine, hold your head up, let your shoulders relax in their sockets and distribute your weight evenly on both feet, these actions alone will take your confidence to another level.

It's important to connect with your internal symbol of confidence regularly through each day, even if you are feeling good anyway. You want this connection to become instantly available and feel like second nature. You know how an action can seem clumsy until you become adept at it? It might be driving or learning a sport or playing a game. Practice is what makes it easier and more enjoyable. Connecting with your confidence is just like that. What makes it much easier, though, is that the only skill you

require for this is the willingness to focus upon it and to feel it. That is much easier than taking up a new sport!

Of course there is another consideration in this 'embracing your confidence' area. You may find you can enter this state when you are on your own, or in company where you are not being challenged. What happens when there is someone else with whom you feel less comfortable?

Let's move to Step 6.

PERSONAL EXAMPLE

Despite my years as an actress and management trainer, I can still find going into a room full of strangers daunting and yet it is something I have to do frequently. I use this exercise daily and I would be lost without it. I am always amused to see which animal will turn up at my side; sometimes they are comical ones that I interpret as, 'Whatever you are doing, however serious the subject, remember to have a laugh too!'

Step 6

....

Saying 'No'

Have you noticed that confident people have no problem in saying 'no' to something they don't want to do? They aren't aggressive and tend not to come across as difficult when they do it. How often do you say 'no'?

There are a few reasons why some people struggle with turning down a request. Do any of these statements ring true for you?

- You don't want to let someone else down.
- You like to be liked and saying 'no' might make you unpopular.
- You fear being seen as a failure or incapable.
- You would feel so guilty if you said 'no'.
- The other person who does it will get all the praise, so you'll be sidelined.

You need to develop a few strategies so that saying
'no', when appropriate, becomes part of your natural state
of confidence. The following suggestions are tools that
you can use irrespective of what drives you to say 'yes'
most of the time.

There are people who can push you off balance.
Their energy can seem like a driving force that you can't
withstand. They don't have to be loud or forceful; some of
the most persuasive people are very quiet and calm, but
their intention is so clear that you feel it as an unstoppable
beam of energy. It can be hard to remain confident when
faced with this.

One simple technique is to ground yourself physically.
Sit or stand in your naturally confident position, weight on

both feet. Remember your energy is heavy and solid. Then imagine you have roots growing out of the soles of your feet, anchoring you deep into the ground. No matter what metaphorical pushing you receive, you can't be knocked over because your roots will always keep you on your feet and sturdy. If someone is making you feel bombarded by their behaviour, simply imagine those roots. Make them really thick and long if you need to and embed them deep into the earth's core.

Maintain eye contact with the other person. I don't mean you need to stare at them, but don't look away from them either. Looking into someone else's eyes can be so useful, because I think the eyes never lie. As you listen to the person, notice what is really going on. Are they panicked? Are they struggling to look at you? Are they feeling desperate? Use this time to understand them more.

You might want to deflect some of their energy back towards them. Picture yourself sitting in a really shiny suit of armour that they can't penetrate with their energy. Notice the effect your imaginary suit of armour has on them.

Then when you respond, start with consideration of their position. Use empathy, acknowledge their concern without letting it consume you. Remember you have your suit of armour to stop you taking their energy back into you. You have your own energy; you don't need theirs as well.

Now consider your reason for saying 'no'. Why is it fair? What are the sensible reasons for your refusal? State them. You may find

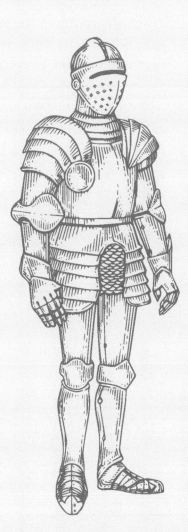

pushback to what you say, so be prepared to repeat them. As you do so, remember to connect with your symbol of confidence. There are good, justifiable reasons for your 'no'. Make sure you express them. Reiterate your appreciation of the person's situation and clarify your own position at the end.

If, during your interaction with someone else, you feel your resolve start to weaken, not because you necessarily agree with what the other person is saying but because you feel sorry for them, or start to feel guilty about your refusal, take a deep breath. Connect with your inner symbol of confidence. Check with yourself if you are caving in through habit, rather than for a good reason. Focus on

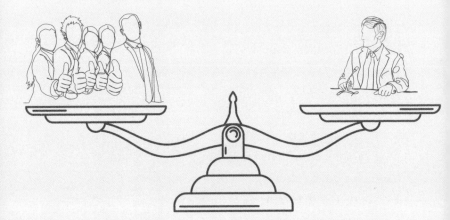

breathing deeply. Feel your confidence symbol growing and glowing inside you. Remember it is fine to remain empathetic towards the other person; it is not fine to lose connection with your own innate state of confidence and find yourself morphing into someone who isn't you.

I have suggested a lot of tools for you to use in the last few paragraphs. Please reread them now to help embed them in your subconscious. You may find this short acronym useful in remembering how to say 'no' effectively and fairly:

R = Roots
E = Eye contact
A = Armour
L = Level-headed.

The 'level-headed' aspect is about levelling off your needs as well as theirs, while staying connected to your confidence symbol inside. It's important to realize there is nothing arrogant about saying 'no' when we are doing so for the right reasons. And I like using the word 'REAL' to focus upon, because being confident IS being real.

I understand that for some of you these four actions may not be the easiest to do initially, particularly if you are someone who has spent a great deal of your life always saying 'yes'. Changing any ingrained habit can take time and perseverance.

So, if you tend to fall into the trap of always saying 'yes' to everything, here is your challenge. Every day, find one thing to which you can say 'no'. It doesn't have to be something major, especially in the beginning. It could be as simple as refusing a drink when you don't want one. When you start to acknowledge how often you say 'yes' to everything, then it becomes easier to choose your moments to say 'no'.

Now let's put everything you have learned in this step into a simple meditation that you can practise right now before you try it in reality.

STEP 6:
THE SAYING 'NO' EXERCISE

Think of a situation where you often give in and say 'yes' even though you know you should be saying 'no'. Are you normally standing or sitting when this happens? Can you stand or sit in the place where it occurs without being interrupted for a few minutes? Breathe deeply for a moment, standing or sitting upright, head up, shoulders down.

Now, keeping your eyes open, imagine that the person you give in to is in front of you. Does their energy immediately make you feel daunted? Go on, ground yourself. Feel your feet resting firmly on the ground, very heavy and solid. Keeping the person's image in front of you, imagine long roots coming from the soles of your feet, snaking into the earth. The roots are long and make you feel very anchored, very firm. Nothing can knock you over.

Imagine you are looking the person in the eyes. You're still feeling solid, so you feel safe. Their eyes are looking back at you and you don't need to break your gaze. By looking into their eyes, you can see them with all their vulnerability too.

Now imagine them talking to you, stating their needs.

Feel their energy, how they move and how they speak in front of you. You are still feeling solid, with the roots coming from the soles of your feet, and your eyes looking into theirs, but now you are picturing yourself in a suit of armour.

It is a full suit of body armour, shiny and new, which covers your whole body. You feel very comfortable in it, very protected.

Now take in their words and what they need. Take your focus on to your symbol of confidence and feel it glowing within you. Consider their words.

Think about their needs and about yours. Why should you say 'no'? Where is the benefit for both of you?

When you feel ready, speak your 'no' out loud and tell them your reasons. If you want to imagine them pushing back and how you will respond, do that too. Take your time. Don't rush your words. Speak slowly. Remember to breathe.

You may find your animal of confidence appearing beside you as you speak. That is fine. It is there as an outward symbol of added support.

Notice how calm you feel, now you have spoken. Imagine the person accepting your words, your reasoning. Thank them for it.

When you are ready, let the image of them in front of you fade into nothingness. Blink to check they have gone. Take a couple of deep, satisfied breaths. Well done!

HELPFUL HINT

Always allow yourself to have fun in your mini-meditations. Do you fancy giving your armour an outrageously bright colour? Go for it! No one else will 'see' it but you. And you may find quirky animals coming to support you from time to time. Welcome them and consider what their unusual energy offers you.

Going through this meditation first will give you more confidence when you face the person in reality. You may find that through using your 'REAL' acronym, the resistance you anticipate from them doesn't materialize. Just as their energy can affect you, so your 'REAL' energy can affect them in return.

Lastly for this step, remember that your saying 'no' is for a reason that is valid and important. True confidence is knowing your place in the world and not needing others to validate or reward you.

PERSONAL EXAMPLE

People often think I have no trouble saying 'no' because my general demeanour tends to exude confidence. In fact, I have been challenged on many occasions over the years and continue to be now. The only difference for me now is that as soon as I feel daunted, I have an automatic response of, 'Yes, I feel that way but it's okay, I can do this' and that reassures me. I'd love to be able to say I short-circuit the insecure moment altogether, but that wouldn't be true. And I think it is important to acknowledge our human frailty because otherwise we could come across as arrogant or cold. It is better to admit that we 'feel the fear and do it anyway' as opposed to pretending we never feel it. Oh, and sometimes my armour takes on a bright pink hue, because it makes me feel wonderfully feminine AND strong at the same time!

Step 7

· · · · · · · · · · · ·

Taking It
Forward

Now you have myriad tools at your disposal to help you move forward in your life, full of confidence, full of the ability to see who you really are, as opposed to what others may think of you or want you to be. Go back and look through the first artwork you made, with thoughts about the word 'confidence'. How much have your opinions changed now? You may want to make a fresh drawing.

This last step is to consider the areas of your life that will benefit most from your newly discovered confidence. The reason I say this is because deciding you will feel confident about everything, all the time, puts a lot of pressure on you.

Accessing this confidence inside you is a skill at which you will become more and more adept as you practise it. Your confidence symbol and wherever it resides inside you is always going to be part of you.

The more you focus on it, the stronger it becomes. Your confidence animal will always be with you; you just need to visualize it when you want it to appear. Remember to welcome different animals into your world, as and when they emerge. Enjoy them all. Whatever other sights/sounds/images/tastes work for you, they will become easily available the more you use them.

But if you set yourself the task of being confident in every aspect of life, you may find it tiring and ultimately hard work. Remember, you learn best when having fun, so do keep enjoying yourself.

Broadly speaking, there are two main areas of our life where confidence affects us most: at work and at play. Some people are naturally confident in the workplace and not so comfortable in personal circumstances. Others are the opposite. Which is true for you?

Which aspect of work or play would you like to influence most, in a positive way?

Be honest with yourself. Choose just one area. You might want to make a list of what you would like to tackle first, but don't make it a long list – no more than three.

Now go through the meditations and exercises in this book and notice what happens for you with the first area you want to look at. Make a note of your results. When you focus intently on one specific area, you will end up with clear information that you can use.

As you will appreciate now, any lack of confidence you feel stems from an experience in your past. Once you access that and clear it, you can move forward.

It's a good idea to make notes in Step 7 of your Confidence Plan, noting what tools help you most for different issues. If you find yourself having a 'down' day or a moment when your confidence ebbs, please be kind to yourself. We are allowed to be human — we can't be 'perfect' all the time.

It may be a constant support to have your confidence symbol with you as a reminder: draw it, make it your screensaver, have an object in that shape near you. If having your animal present makes you feel confident, keep its energy alive in whatever way feels right for you.

It is often said that we are all work in progress, but my attitude is that we are also play in progress, so do remember to embrace both! Now please enjoy this final mini-meditation which follows.

STEP 7:
THE 'I AM CONFIDENCE' MEDITATION

Find somewhere quiet to sit or lie on your own, close your eyes and concentrate on your breathing for a few minutes. Let yourself relax.

Take your attention inside your body, to your confidence symbol. Feel it pulsing gently inside you. Now, as you breathe in, feel your breath go into the symbol. As you breathe out, see the symbol expand. Repeat. Do this gently. You don't need to take deep breaths. Just feel comfortable. Your confidence symbol is expanding like a beautiful balloon being blown up. As it grows in size, notice how your confidence level keeps expanding too.

Continue breathing into the symbol and allowing it to become bigger and bigger. Now start to feel your own body melt into the symbol, until you and the symbol are one entity. There is no 'you' and 'your symbol', just you AS your confidence symbol.

This is a profound feeling. You are not connecting with something, you are just 'being'. This is your true state of confidence. This is who you truly are. This is effortless. You pulse with energy that is comfortable. You glow with it. You are solid and secure and need nothing more. Bask in that nice feeling.

Stay in this state for a while. Notice how your breathing feels effortless and comfortable too.

When you are ready, you are going to begin

shrinking your symbol again. So as you breathe in, the symbol begins to deflate.

As you breathe out, the symbol settles again. Repeat this process. Keep doing it until your symbol returns to its normal size.

Then let your symbol nestle back into its usual resting place in your body. Give it a gentle pat. It feels comfortable. You will realize that you feel content to have it reduced back to its usual size and place within you, but equally content to know you have the ability to expand it as and when you need to do so.

Then take some time to ground yourself again. Your body feels wonderfully heavy and comfortable. Your feet are solid against the ground. Don't rush to open your eyes and when you do, focus on an object in the room and wait a while before you get up. Notice how upright your posture is and how good you feel as you continue your day.

When you finish this final exercise, I hope you feel a profound sense of confidence from deep inside that radiates outwards in a warm glow.

Understand now that you can expand and retract your confidence, given your situation and needs, and really embrace the knowledge that it is always within you.

So as you go about your daily life, keep reminding yourself that confidence is WHO you are; no longer do you need to think of it as an attitude or a belief you have to adopt.

You ARE confidence. Enjoy it!

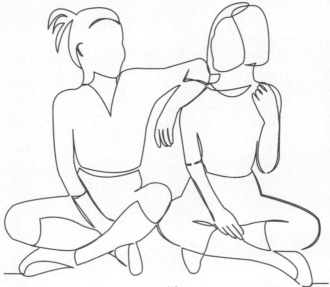

PERSONAL EXAMPLE

Confidence is a joyous state of being that allows you to be the best you can be. One of the biggest benefits of living in a state of confidence is that it enables you to support others in a profound way. When you help others, not because you need acknowledgement or reward in order to make you feel better, but purely because you want to empower others, people can sense your freedom of energy. It makes them want to be the best they can be. It becomes a cycle of positivity that expands and encompasses so many possibilities. Have a wonderful time discovering this.

Epilogue

It's been a pleasure sharing my confidence 'tools' with you and I wish you carefree confidence for the future in all areas of your life. If *Build Your Confidence* has helped you, please share it with others. You may want to consider a further title in this series too: *A Guide to Happiness*.

May your confidence increase and expand in every way, allowing you to enjoy being who you truly are.

Confidence Plan

Step 1

After playing **The Confidence Word Game**, how would you describe your attitude to confidence now?

Describe your experiences of **The Confidence Meditation**:

Images

Sounds

Smells

Tastes

Feelings

Describe your **Confidence Animal**:

Reasons why you choose to stay unconfident:

Describe in detail your **Core of Confidence Symbol**:

Where does it reside in you?

Any other associated experiences:

Step 4

Where does your lack of confidence reside in you?

How did you break it down/clear it?

Describe your unconfident stance and how it makes you feel:

Describe your confident stance and how it makes you feel:

How did your clapping make you feel?

How did putting the pencil between your teeth make you feel?

When might you use these techniques in future?

How do I feel when I imagine roots growing out of the soles of my feet?

When can I use this?

How often do I maintain eye contact with others?

How can I do this more?

Step 6

What does my suit of armour look/feel like?

When do I need to use it?

Why do I struggle to say 'no'?

When do I most need to do this?

What happened when I practised saying 'no'?

What is most helpful for me to remember when I say 'no'?

Step 7

What three experiences do I want to work on now?